GW01368217

SCIENCE THROUGH THE SEASONS

SUMMER ON THE FARM

Janet Fitzgerald

Hamish Hamilton · London

Acknowledgement
I should like to express my gratitude to the schools, teachers and children with whom I have worked, and with whose help I have gained the experience and confidence needed to write this series. I am particularly indebted to those schools which allowed photographs to be taken as the children carried out their investigations. Thanks are also due to Chris Fairclough for some of the excellent photographs illustrating the texts.

Janet Fitzgerald

The publishers would like to thank the following for supplying transparencies for this book:

Heather Angel 8, 14; Ardea 11, 18, 20; Alan Beaumont 13 (below); Nick Birch 13 (above); Bruce Coleman title page, 20 (left), 22; Chris Fairclough back cover, 6, 7, 9, 10, 12, 15–17, 19, 21, 23, 24; Farmer's Weekly front cover, 26, 27; Wales Scene 25.

Author's note

Books in this series are intended for use by young children actively engaged in exploring the environment in the company of a teacher or parent. Many lifelong interests are formed at this early age, and a caring attitude towards plants, animals and resources can be nurtured to become a mature concern for conservation in general.

The basis for all scientific investigation rests on the ability to observe closely and to ask questions. These books aim to increase a child's awareness so that he or she learns to make accurate observations. First-hand experience is encouraged and simple investigations of observations are suggested. The child will suggest many more! The aim is to give children a broad base of experience and 'memories' on which to build for the future.

HAMISH HAMILTON CHILDREN'S BOOKS

Published by the Penguin Group
27 Wrights Lane, London W8 5TZ, England
Viking Penguin Inc, 40 West 23rd Street, New York, New York 10010, U.S.A.
Penguin Books Australia Ltd, Ringwood, Victoria, Australia
Penguin Books Canada Ltd, 2801 John Street, Markham, Ontario, Canada L3R 1B4
Penguin Books (N.Z.) Ltd, 182–190 Wairau Road, Auckland 10, New Zealand

Penguin Books Ltd, Registered Offices: Harmondsworth, Middlesex, England

First published in Great Britain 1989 by
Hamish Hamilton Children's Books

Copyright © 1989 by Janet Fitzgerald

1 3 5 7 9 10 8 6 4 2

All rights reserved. Without limiting the rights under copyright reserved above, no part of this publication may be reproduced, stored in or introduced into a retrieval system or transmitted, in any form or by any means (electronic, mechanical, photocopying, recording or otherwise), without the prior written permission of both the copyright owner and the above publisher of this book.

British Library Cataloguing in Publication Data
Fitzgerald, Janet
  Summer on the farm
  I. Title II. Series
  338.1

ISBN 0–241–12581–2

Printed in Great Britain by William Clowes Ltd, Beccles & London

Contents

Haymeadows	6
Clover	8
Butterflies	10
Strawberries	12
Flowers in the cornfield	14
Harvesting	16
Rabbits	18
Birds	20
Sheep shearing	22
Agricultural show	24
Looking at . . . machines on the farm	26
For teachers and parents	28
Extension activities	28
Index	31

It is summer on the farm and haymeadows are cut.

How many different flowers are in the grass?

What colours are the flowers?

Look at the shapes of the flowers.

Go for a walk and collect
four different grasses.

How did you choose the grasses?

How are the grasses different?

Make a careful drawing of each grass.

It is summer on the farm and clover grows in the grass.

It has a strong sweet scent.

Insects like the colour and the scent.

What colour is the clover?

Find some clover on the lawn or school field.

Collect one plant with roots and leaves.

Look to see how the leaves grow on the clover plant.

Draw the shape of the leaves.

Look at the roots.

9

It is summer on the farm and we see meadow brown butterflies.

What colour is the butterfly?

Look at the marks on the wings and the shape of the body.

Sit quietly in the garden or park on a sunny day.

Watch for butterflies.

How does the butterfly rest on the plant?

How are the wings folded?

How can the butterfly see?

It is summer on the farm and some farmers grow strawberries.

How does the farmer protect the strawberries?

Can you see the seeds of the strawberry?

What will happen to the strawberries after they are picked?

Lots of soft fruits ripen in the summer.

Pick or buy a few summer fruits.

Look to see if they are the same.

Is the colour the same?

What about the shape?

Do they taste the same?

It is summer on the farm and poppies and daisies grow in the cornfield.

What colours are the flowers in the cornfield?

Is it easy to see them in the crop?

Watch to see which flowers insects like best.

Why do the insects like these flowers?

Paint a picture of the faces of some of the flowers.

Are there any interesting shapes or patterns?

It is summer on the farm and grain crops are harvested.

What is left when the harvester has passed?
Where will the small creatures and insects go?
What will happen to the grain now?

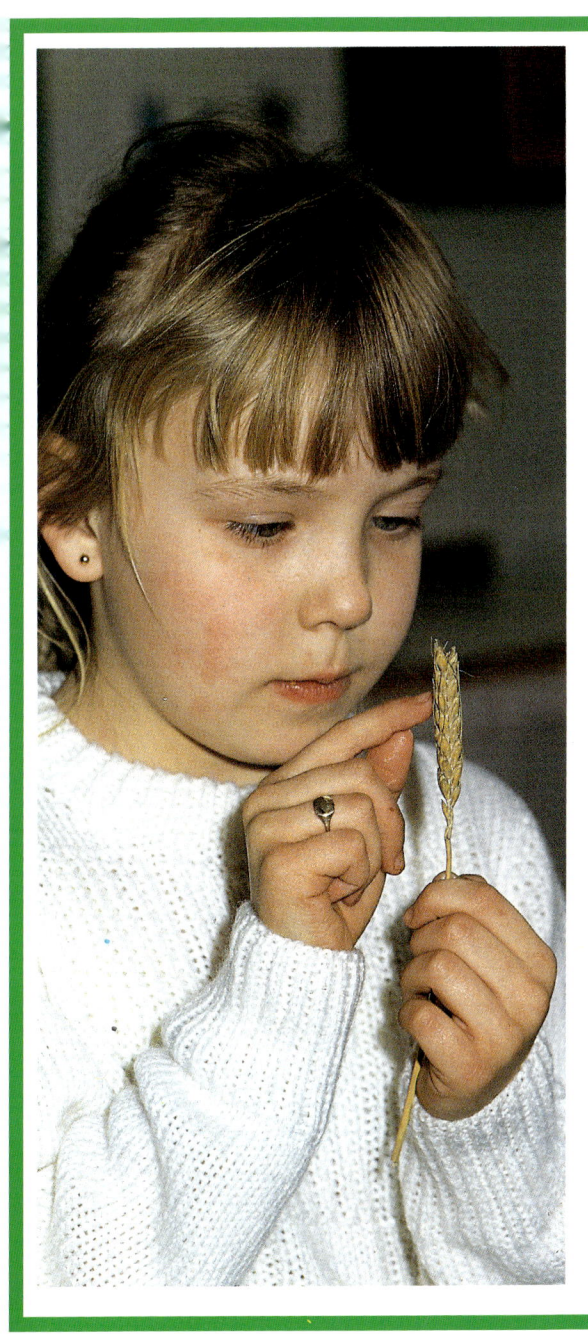

Collect some 'ears'
of barley and wheat.

Look to see if the
'ears' are different.

Rub the 'ears'
between your hands.

Collect the grains.

How many grains
are in each 'ear'?

It is summer on the farm and rabbits run in the cornfields.

Why do the rabbits like the cornfields?

Where will the rabbits hide when the corn is cut?

Rabbits make good pets for home or school.
They should live in a special hutch.

The rabbits must have plenty of room.

They like to run about and nibble grass.

How can we make sure that
the rabbits can do this?

It is summer on the farm and sparrows eat the grain.

Look at the sparrow's beak.

Is it a good shape for eating grain?

Are there any other animals which like to eat grain?

Birds often eat young shoots and ripe crops.

Farmers try to frighten them away without harming them.

Make your own bird scarer.

Will it be big, brightly coloured, noisy, or frightening?

It is summer on the farm and farmers are sheep shearing.

Why does the farmer clip the sheep in summer?

What will the wool be used for?

How do you think the sheep will feel without their wool?

Collect four different balls of knitting wool.
Cut a length and look at the strands.

Will the wool stretch?

Find out if the wool is strong.

Measure four lengths and tie weights to the ends.

It is summer on the farm and cows are taken to the show.

At the show the cows must look their best.

Why does the farmer take animals to the show?

How will the farmer make sure that they are well looked after?

At the show everyone takes something they are proud of.

Some people take flowers they have grown.

The flowers are chosen
for colour, size or scent.

Make a flower display.

How will you choose the best flowers?

Looking at . . .

. . . machines on the farm

If you go to a farm you will see lots of different machines.

Tractors have special wheels and tyres for going over rough ground.

They can pull
other machines,
like ploughs.

Combine harvesters cut
the wheat and separate
out the grain.

Try to find out about
other machines on the
farm.

27

For teachers and parents

We all recognise that children possess an insatiable curiosity about the rich environment and exciting experiences around them. For this reason they have a natural affinity for science and a basic inclination to explore and discover the world in which we live. We need to foster this sense of wonder by encouraging a scientific way of thinking in the early years. Children's own experience of the immediate environment will provide a natural starting point.

Through science children can evolve an active process of enquiry. This begins with observation (including sorting, comparing, ordering and measuring) and continues with asking questions, devising practical investigations, predicting outcomes, controlling variables, noting results, and perhaps modifying the original question in the light of discovery. The books in this series offer suggestions for engaging young children in this sort of active enquiry by relating seasonal change to familiar surroundings.

Extension activities

Pages 6–7
Discover where different types of grasses like to grow. Are there some which like dry, wet, sunny or shady places? What happens if grass is never mowed? Look at grass verges or open spaces in woodland. Investigate the flowers and seeds of grasses and compare with other plants. Find out where the farmer stores the hay, how it is kept for winter feeding and which animals it is used for.

Pages 8–9
Compare clover with other plants readily found in grassland (e.g. buttercup, dandelion, daisy, plantain). Look at the shape, colour and pattern of the leaves. Study the insects which visit clover. Look carefully at the flower of the clover noticing the shape and shading of colour.

Pages 10–11
If possible, follow the life cycle of the butterfly. It is easy to obtain eggs or chrysalids from butterfly farms and incubate your own. Discover the differences between butterflies and moths. Do they fly in the same way and at similar times? Do they have a similar life cycle?

Pages 12–13
Grow some strawberry plants and discover how new plants grow. Look to see where the leaves are attached to the plant and where the fruit forms. Some farmers protect the fruit with straw but is there any other method used? Compare the strawberry plant with the raspberry. Is there an advantage to growing on canes? Consider which crop is easiest to harvest. Discuss ways of using soft fruit and ways of preserving (e.g. bottling, canning, jam making, pie fillings, wine).

Pages 14–15
Discuss the use of the term 'weed' and decide when a flower is called a weed. Visit a cornfield and see where most of the wild flowers are growing. If the flowers are cut with the crop discuss how they will grow again next year. Some of them may have creeping or tangled roots which break up and produce new plants. Decide which ones will survive well.

Pages 16–17
Collect some barley or wheat grains. Try grinding the grain to make flour, between two flat stones, with a rolling pin or a coffee grinder. Discuss the amount of grain needed to make a bag of flour. If possible visit a mill to watch grain being ground and buy some flour to compare with flour from a shop. Look at the different sorts of bread. Compare leavened and unleavened breads. Make a chart showing the different breads people prefer.

Pages 18–19
Consider the special features of the rabbit. Why does it need large ears and a white tail? Make a close study of a pet rabbit. Look at the nose and whiskers. What do the whiskers do? Look at the rabbit's eyes for colour and shape. Does it have eyelids? Watch the rabbit move and consider the length of front and back legs. Look closely at the feet. Compare the rabbit with other pets, e.g. guinea pig.

Pages 20–21
Discover what other means a farmer has for protecting his crops. Are there other birds which damage crops e.g. crows, pigeons. Investigate other animals which eat grain, such as mice. Try to find out when the birds visit the fields. Is it mostly early in the morning or late at night? Does it make a difference if it is a sunny or dull day?

Pages 22–23
Most people think that woollen clothes will keep us warm. Investigate this claim by comparing woollen socks, nylon socks and cotton socks. Place a plastic bottle full of warm water in each and feel to see if the warmth comes through. Leave the bottles in the socks and test frequently to see which socks are retaining the heat. Try different coloured socks, thick socks and thin socks. Be careful not to change too many variables each time. Look at other fabrics. Consider how people dress to suit different climates.

Pages 24–25
If possible, visit a country show. Investigate the origins of some of the crafts, e.g. corn dollies. Try out some old recipes for jam and cakes. Ask about the animals, how they are prepared for the show and what features will be judged. Some farmers will have travelled many miles to the show. Find out how they have transported their animals and produce. Ask about the significance of colours of rosettes and certificates.

Index

birds   20, 21
butterflies   10, 11

colours   6, 8, 10, 13
cows   16, 17
crops   24

feeding   20
flowers   6, 8, 9
fruit   12–15

grain   16–18, 20
grass   7, 19

insects   8, 15, 16

leaves   9

machines   26, 27

rabbits   18, 19

seeds   12
shapes   6, 9, 10, 13, 15
sheep   22, 23
sparrows   20
strawberries   12, 13

wool   22, 23